BEGINNER'S KNOWLEDGE

CASTLES, PYRAMIDS
and
PALACES

Caroline Young
Illustrated by Colin King

Designed by Steve Page and
Mike Pringle

Edited by Cheryl Evans

Consultants:
L.J. Lockett B.A., M.S.I.O.B. (Director of Construction Studies, Croydon College).
K.G. Davies B.A.(Hons.)Arch. (Lecturer, Croydon College).

Historical consultant:
Dr. A. Millard B.A., Dip.Ed.,
Dip.Arch.,PhD.

Contents

TIGER BOOKS INTERNATIONAL

The story of building

This book follows the story of building from the first Stone Age hut to the skyscrapers of today. It tells you how some of the world's most amazing buildings were built, what they were like inside and who lived in them.

Large and small

On this page are some of the buildings you can read about in this book. They are shown next to each other here so that you can see their different sizes.

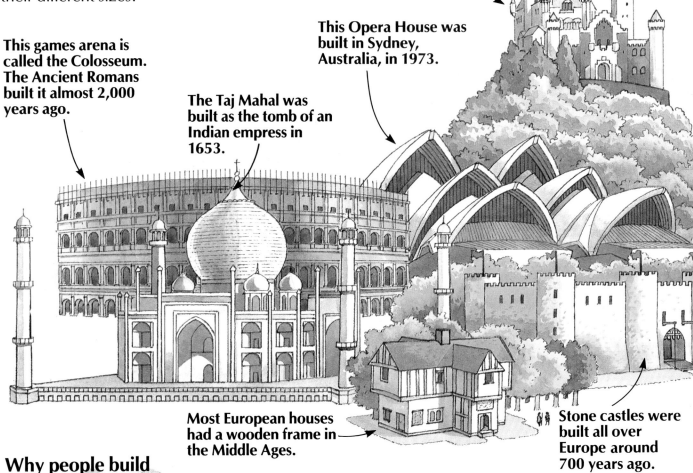

This fairytale castle was built in Germany in 1881.

This Opera House was built in Sydney, Australia, in 1973.

This games arena is called the Colosseum. The Ancient Romans built it almost 2,000 years ago.

The Taj Mahal was built as the tomb of an Indian empress in 1653.

Most European houses had a wooden frame in the Middle Ages.

Stone castles were built all over Europe around 700 years ago.

Why people build

People first built houses to protect themselves from the weather. They used whatever they could find nearby.

Later, people built places where they could worship their god. Every religion had a different building style.

People also built places to work in, such as factories. They needed buildings like theatres to relax in, too.

2

The Empire State Building in New York has 102 storeys. It was built in 1931.

The Eiffel Tower was built of pieces of moulded iron in 1889.

The Ancient Egyptians built the Pyramids as tombs for their kings over 4,500 years ago.

Many huge cathedrals were built in Europe around 800 years ago.

This cathedral was built in Moscow in 1561.

Castles like this were built by Japanese nobles around 450 years ago.

This shrine was built in India 2,000 years ago.

Stone Age men built stone circles, called henges, around 4,000 years ago.

The Ancient Greeks built this marble temple in Athens over 2,000 years ago.

Three building mixtures

Three mixtures are important in the story of building. They are called cement, mortar and concrete. When they dry, they set hard and stick bricks and stones together.

Cement was first made by burning limestone until it became powder. When water was added, cement set hard. Today, clay and chalk are burnt.

When cement is mixed with sand and water, it makes a paste called mortar. Mortar is spread between stones or bricks to bond them together firmly.

Many modern builders use a mixture called concrete. Concrete is made of small stones, sand, cement and water.

The first buildings

Thousands of years ago, people moved from place to place following the animals they hunted. When people started farming the land, they also began building houses.

Hunting huts

The first hunters slept in the open or in caves. If there was no shelter, they built huts from whatever they found nearby.

A group of hunters built huts like these 300,000 years ago, on a beach in southern France.

They covered a frame of branches with leaves and grass to keep wind and rain out.

Early houses

Early houses were built of different things, in different ways, all over the world. Here are some examples.

In Russia, hunters stretched mammoth skins over a frame of tusks, bones and branches to make a hut.

In some hot countries, people tied together bundles of reeds to make a hut. They sometimes covered the reeds with mud.

In countries with plenty of trees, houses had a wooden frame. Twigs plastered with mud filled in gaps.

In some countries, builders made houses from bricks of mud and straw. The bricks dried hard in the sun.

Stonehenge

Over 4,000 years ago, farming people in Europe built huge stone circles called henges.

No one is quite sure why. The most famous one is called Stonehenge, in England.

The builders used tools made of animal bones and deer antlers.

The stones lying across the upright stones are called lintels.

lintel

Stonehenge was re-arranged three times. It was finally finished about 3,700 years ago.

Stone houses were built in Europe over 4,000 years ago. Some had stone furniture and an entrance tunnel.

Some stones weighed up to 26,000 kg. This is as much as about 370 men.

These stones are called bluestones because they look blue when wet.

bluestone

Some people think Stonehenge was a giant calendar. Sunrise can be seen through different pairs of stones at different times of year.

Floating stones

Wales

England

Experts think some of the stones came from Wales. Rafts made of tree trunks may have carried them to the English coast.

These lumps fit into holes dug in the lintels.

It probably took several hundred men about two weeks to drag each stone from the quarry.

Layers of logs were rolled under the lintel to lift it up. When it was high enough, the builders pushed it into place with a wooden lever.

pick

How Stonehenge was built

People think that the stones were cut from rock and dragged 32km from the quarry on a wooden sledge.

Logs and smaller stones were piled up under the stone until it could be pushed into its hole with a wooden lever.

The builders heaved the stone upright. They pushed rocks around the bottom of the stone to keep it in place.

Pyramid builders

The first great builders lived in the East. The Ancient Egyptians built the pyramids over 4,500 years ago.

They were tombs for their kings, called Pharaohs. Almost 500 years earlier, the people living near the Tigris and

Euphrates rivers built huge cities. Their temples were on top of sacred mud-brick platforms called ziggurats.

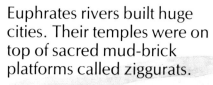

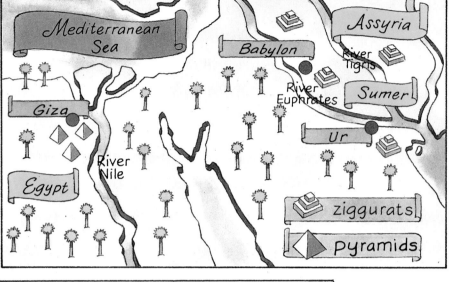

The Pyramids

The Ancient Egyptians only used stone for tombs and temples. The Pharaohs controlled the building work.

The pyramids were supposed to keep the Pharaoh's body safe forever. This one was built around 4,500 years ago for the Pharaoh Khafra.

Each pyramid probably took the Egyptians about 20 years to build.

Ziggurats

This ziggurat stood in the ancient Sumerian city of Ur. It was built over 4,000 years ago. The core was solid mud, with baked mud bricks on the outside.

Some ziggurats had as many as seven layers.

The temple was on the highest layer.

Woven reed mats between layers of bricks made the walls stronger.

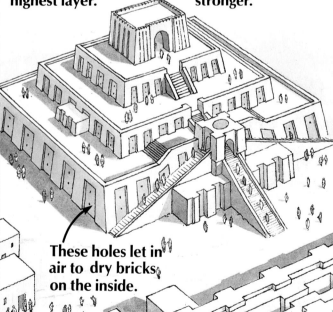

These holes let in air to dry bricks on the inside.

Most people in Ur lived in flat-roofed mud brick houses. They built canals which filled with water when the river Euphrates flooded. This kept their houses safe from the water.

Wooden rockers lifted the stone blocks.

rocker

A mixture of oil and water was poured under the rollers to help them move smoothly up the ramp.

ramp

How a pyramid was built

The builders checked that the building area was completely flat by measuring the level of water in shallow trenches. Men dragged each block from quarries near Giza on wooden sledges. Each one weighed about 2.5 tonnes.

The builders hauled the block up ramps of earth and mud bricks until it reached the space it had to fill.

You can see inside this finished pyramid.

The limestone for the pyramid's coating was floated across the Nile on rafts during the summer, when the river flooded the land.

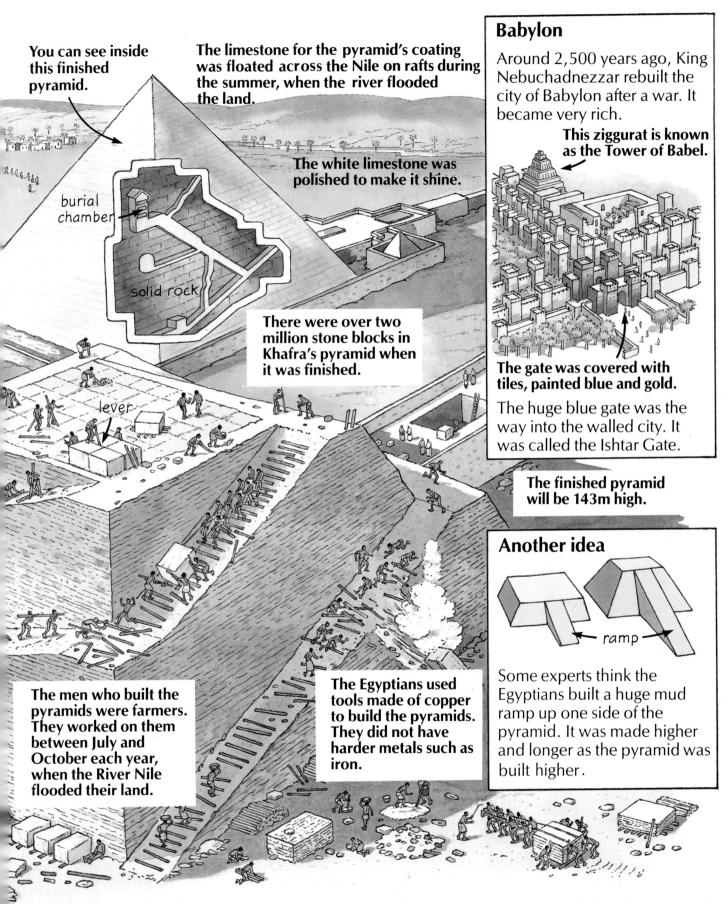

burial chamber

solid rock

The white limestone was polished to make it shine.

There were over two million stone blocks in Khafra's pyramid when it was finished.

lever

The men who built the pyramids were farmers. They worked on them between July and October each year, when the River Nile flooded their land.

The Egyptians used tools made of copper to build the pyramids. They did not have harder metals such as iron.

Babylon

Around 2,500 years ago, King Nebuchadnezzar rebuilt the city of Babylon after a war. It became very rich.

This ziggurat is known as the Tower of Babel.

The gate was covered with tiles, painted blue and gold.

The huge blue gate was the way into the walled city. It was called the Ishtar Gate.

The finished pyramid will be 143m high.

Another idea

ramp

Some experts think the Egyptians built a huge mud ramp up one side of the pyramid. It was made higher and longer as the pyramid was built higher.

The block was smoothed into shape with tools and then pushed into its place with wooden levers.

The ramps got higher as the pyramid grew. When the last block was in place, the builders covered the pyramid

with slabs of white limestone from Tura, across the Nile. The ramps were removed and the pyramid was finished.

The Ancient Greeks

The Ancient Greeks were excellent builders. Around 2,500 years ago, they began rebuilding the city of Athens, which their enemies, the Persians, had ruined.

The Parthenon

This temple in Athens was built to honour Athene, the Greek goddess of war and wisdom.

It is called the Parthenon. It stands on a hill called the Acropolis overlooking Athens.

Crooked or straight?

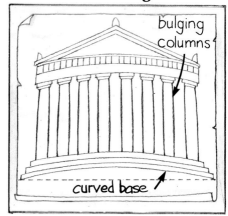

bulging columns

curved base

If the Greeks had built the Parthenon straight, it would look crooked. To avoid this, they made the base curve up 5cm and the columns bulge out slightly.

The Parthenon was the most expensive building in Athens.

The temple took 11 years to build.

The Greeks carved pictures of Athene's life on the Parthenon.

Priests sacrificed animals on an altar near the temple.

Island city

Walls in the palace were decorated with pictures.

People called the Minoans lived on the Greek island of Crete around 4,000 years ago. Their king, Minos, ruled from his palace in the city of Knossos. King Minos lived in luxury in the palace. Farmers brought crops to Knossos to be stored until the king's servants sold them.

Ancient plumbing

This is the queen's bathroom. Knossos had a complicated system of underground stone channels to carry sewage and waste water away.

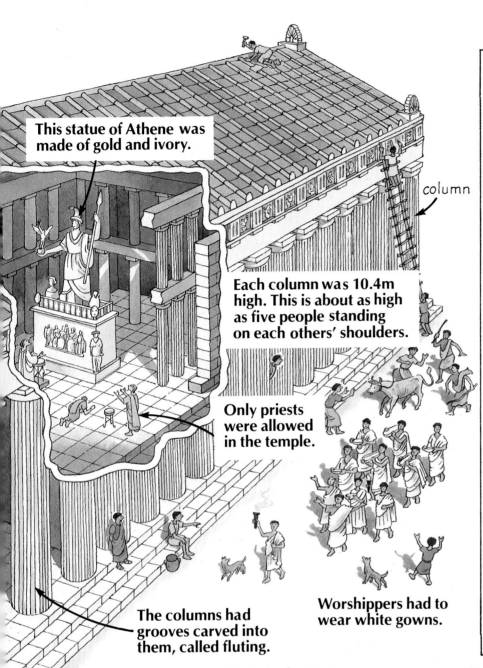

This statue of Athene was made of gold and ivory.

column

Each column was 10.4m high. This is about as high as five people standing on each others' shoulders.

Only priests were allowed in the temple.

The columns had grooves carved into them, called fluting.

Worshippers had to wear white gowns.

Building a column

The builders cut the stone into rough round shapes, called drums, on the ground.

grooves

They carved grooves onto the outside of the block and made a hole in each one.

Wooden pegs were pushed into the hole and the blocks slotted firmly together.

Greek theatres

actors

The priests sat on seats of honour in the front row.

The Greeks built theatres in the open air. They held drama festivals where the actors all wore masks.

The builders chose a hill with gently sloping sides. They cut steps and lined them with marble benches.

Sound effects

tunnel

If a play needed the sound of thunder, round stones were rolled through a tunnel cut under the seats.

9

The Romans

About 2,000 years ago, the city of Rome was at the heart of a vast Empire. It was one of the largest cities of its time. Some of its great buildings still stand today. The Romans built houses, temples, roads and bridges throughout their lands. Roman builders also learnt how to use curved shapes such as arches and domes.

The Colosseum

The Romans built huge arenas called amphitheatres. Men called gladiators fought each other, or wild animals in them. This was the biggest amphitheatre they built, the Colosseum in Rome. It had room for about 50,000 people. The Romans sometimes flooded the Colosseum and watched ships fighting each other in sea battles.

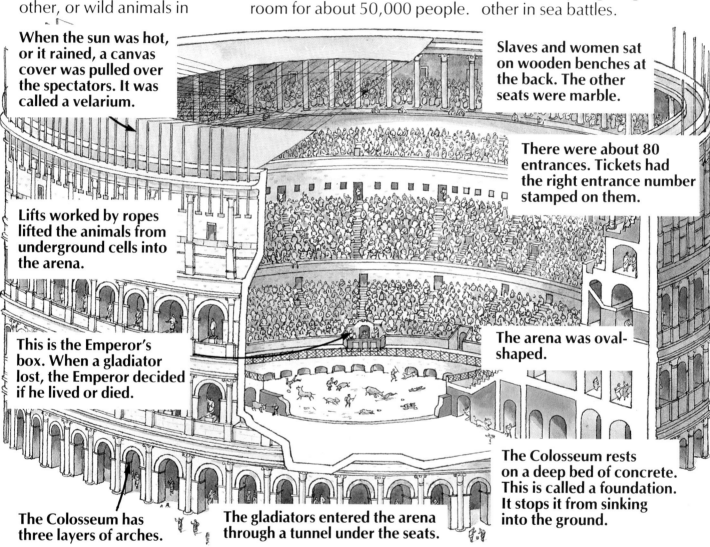

When the sun was hot, or it rained, a canvas cover was pulled over the spectators. It was called a velarium.

Slaves and women sat on wooden benches at the back. The other seats were marble.

There were about 80 entrances. Tickets had the right entrance number stamped on them.

Lifts worked by ropes lifted the animals from underground cells into the arena.

This is the Emperor's box. When a gladiator lost, the Emperor decided if he lived or died.

The arena was oval-shaped.

The Colosseum rests on a deep bed of concrete. This is called a foundation. It stops it from sinking into the ground.

The Colosseum has three layers of arches.

The gladiators entered the arena through a tunnel under the seats.

Building an arch

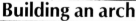

The Romans put an arch-shaped wooden frame on top of two stone pillars or walls.

In the simplest arch, flat stones were tightly packed together around the frame.

Sometimes, a central wedge-shaped keystone held the other stones in place.

Building a dome

The Romans discovered a mixture that became very hard, like concrete, when it dried. They used it to build domes.

The concrete was poured over these wooden moulds.

A frame of square-shaped pieces of wood, called coffers, was put in place over the building. The concrete mixture was poured over the coffers.

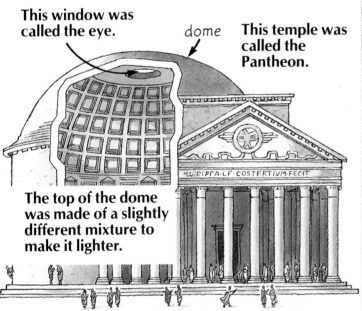

This window was called the eye.

dome

This temple was called the Pantheon.

The top of the dome was made of a slightly different mixture to make it lighter.

MAGRIPPA·LF·COSTERTIVM·FECIT

When the mixture dried, the framework was taken down. A hard concrete dome now stood over the building.

Life in Rome

Houses in the city were expensive because land to build on was limited.

hypocaust

Wealthy Romans had large houses with courtyards. In winter, warm air from fires swirled under the floors. This method of heating was called a hypocaust.

Several poorer families lived in blocks like these. They were made of bricks and wood and built in narrow streets.

Transporting water

When the builders took the frame away, the stones stayed in the arch shape.

Three layers of arches made the aqueduct stronger.

The Romans built bridges called aqueducts to carry water to cities.

This aqueduct at Nîmes in France is nearly 50km long. It is lined with lead.

Fortress castles

Kings and lords built castles to protect them from enemies. They had to be strongly made and difficult to attack. Many were on top of hills or surrounded by water.

Early castles

Hundreds of carts full of earth were needed to build a motte.

motte

bailey

Castles like this were built in Europe 900 years ago. A wooden tower stood on a mound of earth, called a motte. The area inside the fence was called the bailey.

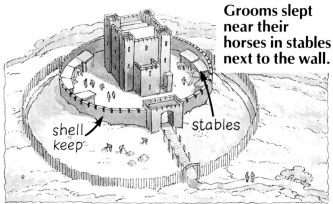

Grooms slept near their horses in stables next to the wall.

shell keep

stables

Later, castles were built of stone which lasted longer than wood. An outer wall, called the shell keep, protected the people and buildings inside from attack.

Medieval castle

Between 1277 and 1285, King Edward I of England built several great castles like this one to defend his kingdom.

Archers fired arrows through these slits in the wall. It was difficult for enemy arrows to hit them.

portcullis

The gatehouse had to be well protected. It had a thick wooden door, spiked gate called a portcullis and a drawbridge.

drawbridge

Builders put a mortar, or paste, made of sand, burnt chalk and water between stones to stick them together.

mortar

Some castles had secret tunnels so that people could escape if the castle was surrounded by enemies.

Building a castle

A man called a master mason drew the plans for a castle. He also found the men to do the building work.

The men moved from building one castle to another. 900 men took about seven years to build a castle like this.

Stone for the walls came from quarries nearby. Men called stonecutters used picks and chisels to cut it into blocks.

Krak des Chevaliers

Between 1096 and 1291, Christians and Muslims fought for the Holy Land in wars called Crusades.

Enemies can be seen from every side of these round towers.

An aqueduct carried water into the castle.

aqueduct

This windmill ground grain for bread.

Both sides built castles. The Christian knights built this one in Syria. It is called Krak des Chevaliers. It has steep outer walls and was very difficult for enemies to conquer.

This part of the tower juts out. It is called a machicolation. Rocks or stones could be thrown onto attackers through these holes.

crane

The stone walls only rose by about 3m a year.

scaffolding

This wooden crane lifted stone blocks on ropes. A man moved the wheel by walking round inside it.

Building stopped during the winter because of wet, cold weather.

Many castles had a ditch called a moat around them.

moat

Carpenters built a frame of poles, ramps and ladders called scaffolding as the stone walls grew higher.

When all the stone-work was finished, the carpenters added wooden floorboards, furniture and wooden roof beams.

Inside a castle

The lord, his family and hundreds of soldiers and servants lived in a castle.

The Great Hall was the most important room in a castle. The lord saw visitors and held great feasts there.

Castles were cold and draughty places. Tapestries hung on the walls, and rugs of woven rushes helped keep it warm.

Many castles had stone toilets built into the outer walls. Some emptied into a pit, which a servant had to clean out.

Inside the castle

Enemies often camped outside the castle and stopped food, water and fuel going in. This was called a siege.

Cathedrals and churches

Around 800 years ago, people in Europe began building huge churches called cathedrals. They built them to show their love for God and to thank him for making their towns so prosperous. Most townspeople gave money or helped build their cathedral. God was very important in their lives.

Who built a cathedral?

Cathedral builders were craftsmen. This means that they each had a special skill.

An architect drew the plans for the cathedral. He was often a master mason.

Masons made sure that every block was in its correct place. Some carved the stone.

Stone-cutters were paid for each block they cut, so they cut their own mark into it.

Building a cathedral took so long that several generations worked on each one.

The cathedral

Cathedrals like this were built over 700 years ago in France. Some took over 100 years to finish.

Carvings like this decorated cathedral ceilings. They were called roof bosses. Many showed scenes from the Bible.

Stone ribs divided up the ceiling. This is called ribbed vaulting.

The carving in cathedrals often showed good and evil. In this one, a thief is being punished.

spire

Cathedral spires could be seen from far away. Some were over 100m above the ground.

Building a roof this high was dangerous. There were often accidents.

This is the roof over the nave. The nave is 30m high, which is as tall as about 16 men standing on each other's shoulders.

These are flying buttresses. They prop up the nave walls.

The townspeople met friends and discussed business in the cathedral as well as worshipping there.

Stained glass windows

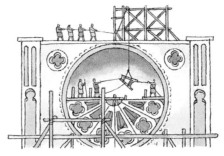

The architect drew a plan of each window. Masons put this plan over the stone and carved the window frame bit by bit.

Cranes lifted each piece into place, so that they formed the right stone pattern. Each of the hundreds of spaces in the

pattern was filled with pieces of coloured glass. The builders used melted lead to seal them together.

These are called pinnacles. Each one was carefully carved by sculptors.

This is the bell-tower. Some bells needed 12 men to ring them.

These round windows are called rose windows.

Gargoyles like this spouted rainwater off the cathedral roof. They were ugly to scare evil spirits away.

Many cathedrals were built of limestone. It was very strong, but quite easy to carve.

Some cathedrals have nearly 200 windows.

scaffolding

Wooden churches

In Scandinavia around 800 years ago, people built wooden churches because they had plenty of timber. They were called stave churches.

carving

This church was built in about 1150 in Norway.

They decorated them with wooden carvings such as dragons' heads. The doorways were often covered with carved pictures.

Mayas, Aztecs and Incas

Three great civilizations used to live in the mountains, jungles and plains of Central and South America. The first were a tribe called the Mayas. They were followed by the Aztecs, and later the Incas in Peru. European explorers conquered them over 450 years ago. The ruins of their beautiful cities can still be seen today.

Central
America

Atlantic
Ocean

Andes
Mountains

South
America

Pacific
Ocean

Peru

■ Mayas
■ Incas
□ Aztecs

The Mayas

The Maya empire lasted for 700 years, until the year 1000.

There were over 20,000 small carvings on this strip of wall.

There were several rows of dark, narrow rooms inside Maya palaces.

This building in the city of Uxmal is known as the Governor's Palace. Experts think it was painted bright colours 1,000 years ago.

Maya builders often covered their buildings with carvings.

The palace was 97m long but only 12m wide.

Only priests and wealthy nobles lived in Maya cities. Most people only came into the city to sell their crops or for religious festivals.

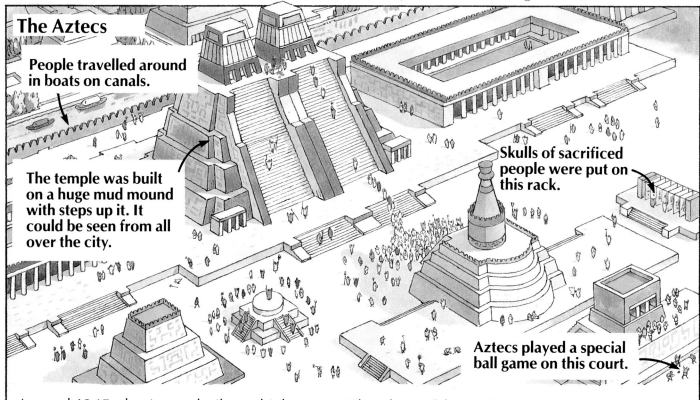

The Aztecs

People travelled around in boats on canals.

The temple was built on a huge mud mound with steps up it. It could be seen from all over the city.

Skulls of sacrificed people were put on this rack.

Aztecs played a special ball game on this court.

Around 1345, the Aztecs built a city on an island in the middle of Lake Texococo. It was called Tenochtitlan, which means 'The place of the prickly pear cactus'. By 1519, it ruled 500 provinces. The Aztec people were very religious. In the city's temples, priests tore out the hearts of human sacrifices to please their gods.

The Incas

About 400 years ago, the Inca tribe ruled an empire that stretched 4,000km.

The Incas built cities like this one high in the Andes Mountains.

Every Inca man had to do the emperor's building work as a kind of tax.

Inca roads

The Incas made rope bridges when the road came to a river.

The Incas also built roads. Their Royal Road of the Andes was so long that it would take over three weeks to walk from one end to the other. The emperor's messengers, called chaksis, ran between mountain towns carrying his orders.

This fortress overlooked the city. It was surrounded by three zig-zagging stone walls.

The Incas did not know how to make wheels, so they had no carts to drag stones.

Up to 20,000 men hauled stone blocks up the mountain side.

Llamas carried food and cloth from town to town.

The stones in the walls fitted together exactly. The Incas used no mortar to join them.

grass

The Incas dug the mountain slopes into shelves called terraces. They grew grain and vegetables there.

llama

Some of these blocks weighed over 100 tonnes.

The Inca emperor

The Incas thought their emperor was the son of the sun god, Inti. Priests served and worshipped him.

Huge gold ornaments decorated the palace rooms. Gold was the sacred metal of the sun god.

This is the palace garden in the city of Cuzco. It was filled with plants and animals made of solid gold.

17

China and Japan

The people of Ancient China and Japan believed that buildings should copy the shapes they saw in nature.

A building wonder

If the wall was attacked, the guards lit a fire to warn the next watchtower.

They used curved roofs and planned beautiful gardens when they built. They also had to make sure that their

buildings were strong enough to survive earthquakes, typhoons and very heavy rain.

The Great Wall is the only building that can be seen from a spacecraft orbiting the Earth.

North China was often attacked by raiders. Nobles built walls to keep them out. About

2,100 years ago, the emperor ordered builders to join all the walls together. They built

the Great Wall of China, which is the longest wall ever built. It is over 5,000km long.

How they built

Some Chinese and Japanese buildings were always built in the same way.

Shinto shrine

Religious shrines like this are still taken down and rebuilt every 20 years in Japan. This way, the building skills and secrets are never forgotten.

This picture shows some of the building methods people used in Ancient China.

Pagodas

Pagoda means 'tower of preciousness'

Layers of wooden brackets share the weight of the roofs.

This tower was called a pagoda. It stood next to a temple. Priests put a sacred object inside it. The first pagodas were timber. Later, they were built of stone.

Himeji Castle

Castles like this one were built in Japan from about 450 years ago, by nobles called daimyos.

The path into the castle had ten gates. These slowed enemies down so that they could be shot at.

Peasants had to grow rice for the daimyo.

The Forbidden City

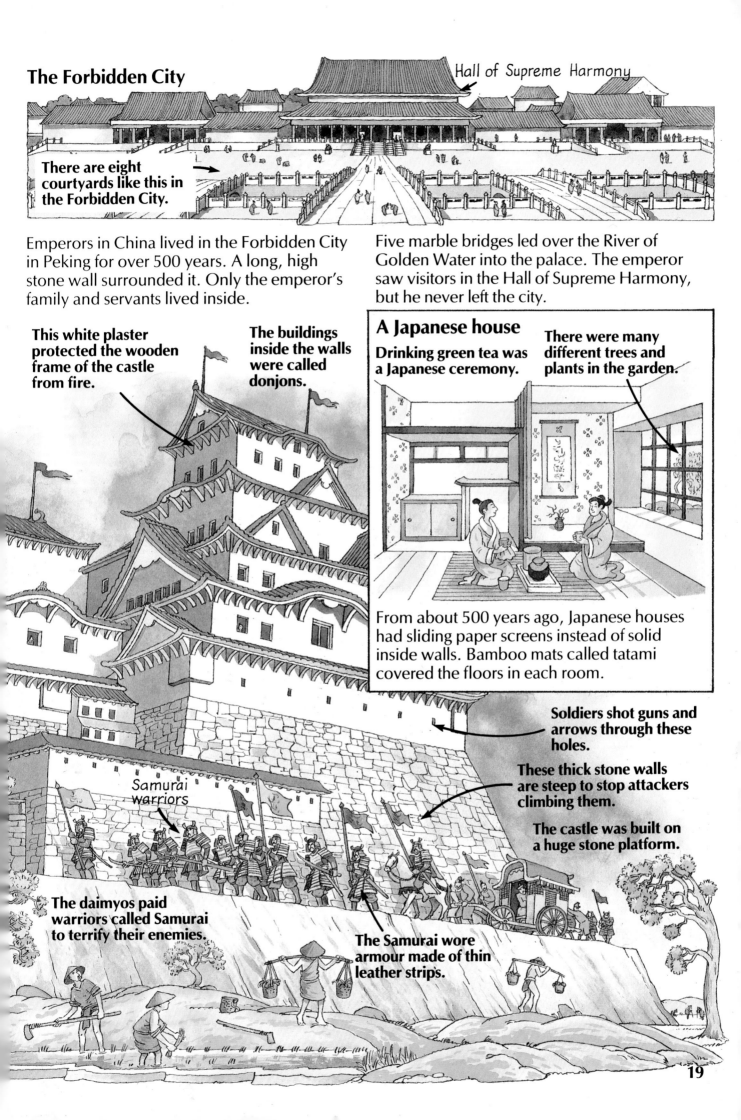

Hall of Supreme Harmony

There are eight courtyards like this in the Forbidden City.

Emperors in China lived in the Forbidden City in Peking for over 500 years. A long, high stone wall surrounded it. Only the emperor's family and servants lived inside.

Five marble bridges led over the River of Golden Water into the palace. The emperor saw visitors in the Hall of Supreme Harmony, but he never left the city.

This white plaster protected the wooden frame of the castle from fire.

The buildings inside the walls were called donjons.

A Japanese house

Drinking green tea was a Japanese ceremony.

There were many different trees and plants in the garden.

From about 500 years ago, Japanese houses had sliding paper screens instead of solid inside walls. Bamboo mats called tatami covered the floors in each room.

Soldiers shot guns and arrows through these holes.

These thick stone walls are steep to stop attackers climbing them.

The castle was built on a huge stone platform.

Samurai warriors

The daimyos paid warriors called Samurai to terrify their enemies.

The Samurai wore armour made of thin leather strips.

Amazing castles

In the 1300s, Europeans began using gunpowder. It could fire cannonballs through a castle's stone walls.

Castles were no longer safe fortresses. People started building them as beautiful homes instead.

The proud lord

The French Duke of Berry asked artists to paint pictures of his castles. This one is of Saumur castle. It was one of twelve in a calendar.

Castles were often the only stone buildings in the area.

It shows what life was like on the Duke's lands. In the month of September, peasants harvested the lord's grapes in front of his beautiful castle.

Fairytale castle

This castle was built in Neuschwanstein in Germany in 1881.

Neuschwanstein Castle was built on top of the ruins of an old castle.

Many German houses have wall-paintings like these.

Ludwig's builders used dynamite to blast away over 6m of solid rock, so that the castle could be built on level ground.

French chateaux

Chambord has over 400 rooms.

In the 1500s, the kings of France began building beautiful castles called chateaux (French for castles). Francis I built this one in Chambord between 1519 and 1547. It had a moat, towers and turrets, but they were just for decoration.

Ludwig had this vase in his bathroom. It was the size of a real swan.

Prince Ludwig

Neuschwanstein castle was built by Prince Ludwig of Bavaria. He wanted to build the most beautiful castle ever.

Building on top of a mountain was slow and difficult. The castle took so long to build that Ludwig only lived in it for six months before he died.

Ludwig was rather strange. He got up at 6pm, ate dinner at ten minutes past midnight, and went to bed at dawn.

There are many different styles of decoration in the castle rooms.

Christian Jank, who planned the castle, was not an architect. He usually worked in the theatre.

gatehouse

The Prince's bed was carved out of wood from walnut trees. It took 17 carpenters four and a half years to finish it.

Only the gatehouse was built of red sandstone. The rest is white limestone.

Tax collectors

Germany was split into small states ruled by barons and princes until 1871.

painted plaster

This castle was the home for four branches of the powerful Eltz family.

Many princes built castles like this one on rocky peaks above rivers. They had a good view of their lands and were very difficult to attack. Passing ships had to pay taxes to the castle's lord.

Fake castles

This is Sham Castle in Bath, England.

There is nothing behind this wall. Follies were built just to look at.

In the 1700s, it was fashionable for rich people to build false castles or ruins, called follies, on their land.

Powerful cities

About 500 years ago, most cities in northern Italy were surrounded by their own states. They were ruled by rich families who had become wealthy by trading with Europe and the East. They were merchants and bankers, and very powerful.

Venice

Venice was one of the richest cities in Italy.

It was built on mud islands in a lagoon, which is a seawater lake separated from the sea by a sandbank.

The ruler of Venice was called the Doge. He lived in this palace.

These decorations were copied from ones seen in the East by sailors from Venice.

Venice has canals instead of roads. People travelled around in these boats, called gondolas.

The Doge's Palace was built of bricks covered with patterns of pink and white stone.

Heavy chains were hung across the opening to the widest canals to keep enemy ships out.

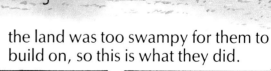

gondola

Building Venice

The first people to settle on the islands in the lagoon were fishermen. They found that the land was too swampy for them to build on, so this is what they did.

They dropped rocks onto the sea bed. Next, they piled layers of wooden planks onto the rocks to make a platform.

If the sea bed was very far down, the builders pushed long tree trunks into it. Then they laid planks on top of them.

The platform was covered with a layer of stone blocks stuck together with cement. Venice was built on this.

Family palaces

Soldiers could drop rocks onto attackers from these holes.

The bell in this bell-tower was rung to warn people in the city of danger.

machicolation

This cathedral next to the palace was the Doge's own private church. It was named St Mark's in 1481. St Mark is the patron saint of Venice.

The ruling families were afraid that their rivals would attack them or that the poor people would riot. Their houses were luxurious inside, but some looked like fortresses from the outside. Soldiers guarded them.

This is the Bridge of Sighs, which led to jail. As prisoners walked across it, they were said to sigh for their lost freedom.

Today, Venice is sinking. Builders are trying to strengthen the mud by injecting concrete into it.

canal

The leaning tower

This bell tower was built in Pisa in 1174. The ground was too soft to support it and one side sank during building.

The tower leans about 1mm further each year.

A staircase with 294 steps leads to the top.

The architect ordered the next four storeys to be built leaning over in the other direction. He hoped this would make the Tower look straight.

A double dome

In 1420, Filippo Brunelleschi won a competition to build the dome of Florence Cathedral. He built a smaller dome inside the main dome, to support it.

Stone ribs made the dome stronger. Brunelleschi's dome was the biggest since the Pantheon in Ancient Rome.

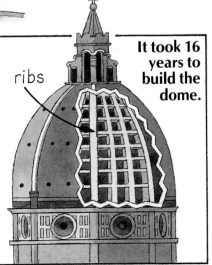

ribs

It took 16 years to build the dome.

Building with wood

About 400 years ago, most houses in northern Europe were made of wood. At this time, many people came to the towns to look for work. Skilful carpenters used timber to build houses for them.

Curved trees

The frame of this house was made of one curved piece of wood, split into two. It is called a cruck frame.

Glass was expensive. Windows were made of small pieces of glass stuck together with strips of lead.

The builders used a rope crane to lift longer pieces of wood.

The inside walls of some of the rooms were covered with sheets of polished wood.

beam

The gaps in the wooden frame were filled with small slices of wood called lath.

Lath was covered with a mixture of clay and straw. White plaster was then smoothed on top.

Hammerbeams

Roofs were held up by pieces of wood, called beams. In large buildings, beams rested on each other to share the roof's weight. These were called hammerbeams.

Wooden wind-power

Six men could cut about 80 tree trunks into planks in one day at this sawmill.

The sawmill could turn to face the wind.

Holland is very flat. It was often flooded by the sea. The people built wooden windmills that pumped water off the land and also ground grain. Some windmills had wind-powered saws and were used to cut wood for building houses.

The carpenter marked each plank to make sure that it was put in the right place when the frame was fitted together.

Wooden Halls

In the 1500s, wealthy families lived in houses like this one. They were called Halls.

Carpenters fitted the pieces of the building together like a huge wooden jigsaw puzzle.

The chimney was made of bricks so that it would not catch fire.

Hard oak pegs to join the frame together.

Curved pieces of wood were also used.

lath

plaster

Carpenters carved the wood with chisels.

pargetting

Nogging

In some countries, builders filled the spaces between wooden beams with bricks. This was called brick nogging.

nogging

thatch

This farmhouse in Germany had a different brick pattern in each panel. Its roof was made of dried straw, called thatch.

The frame for the wall of a small house could be lifted up in one go. This was called rearing a wall.

Builders decorated the wet plaster by pressing a patterned wooden mould or comb onto it. This was called pargetting.

The danger of fire

In 1666, London was a dirty, crowded city. Most people lived in wooden-framed houses several storeys high. The streets were very narrow.

On 1st September 1666 a fire started in a bakery. Five days later, over 13,000 houses had burnt down. A cathedral called St Paul's was ruined.

St. Paul's

After the Fire, London was rebuilt using brick and stone. The famous architect, Sir Christopher Wren built the new stone St Paul's.

Mosques and minarets

In Arabia, about 1,450 years ago, a man called Muhammed began preaching to people about a new religion called Islam.

Its followers were called Muslims. They built richly decorated mosques where they met to pray to Allah, the Muslim God.

A growing empire

A hundred years after Muhammed first preached, the Islamic Empire stretched from the town of Timbuktu in Africa to the edge of India.

Its rulers controlled all the trade in gold, silk and spices between their lands.

A mosque

In 1453, Muslims called Ottoman Turks captured the city of Constantinople. They renamed it Istanbul.

The Ottoman king Suleyman the Magnificent ordered his architect to build this mosque in Istanbul in around 1551.

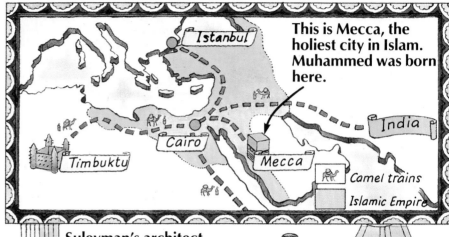

This is Mecca, the holiest city in Islam. Muhammed was born here.

Istanbul

India

Cairo

Timbuktu

Mecca

Camel trains

Islamic Empire

It took about seven years to build a mosque like this one.

A hospital, baths, schools and restaurants were built around the courtyard.

Suleyman's architect was called Sinan. He was in charge of over 470 buildings. 196 still stand today.

This mosque was built of limestone and white marble.

In some Islamic countries, minarets were built in a spiral-shape like this one.

Worshippers washed at this fountain before going in to pray.

Camel trains

The traders lay on sofas under these cool arches.

Camels were fed and watered in the caravanserai.

Traders travelled on camels in groups called caravans. They rested in places called caravanserais.

The high walls kept raiding tribesmen out. The arched roofs kept the sun off so that the building stayed cool.

Small stained glass windows around the base of the dome let in light.

The huge stone columns were wide apart in mosques to leave space for worshippers.

muezzin

column

The holiest place in a mosque is called the mihrab. It faces towards Mecca.

The walls were covered with brightly decorated tiles.

The floor was covered with patterned rugs.

Sheets of lead covered the domes.

These towers are called minarets. A man called a muezzin is calling Muslims to prayers from the top.

Using tiles

Many Muslim buildings were covered with patterned tiles. The tile-makers were skilled at using bright colours.

Islamic builders wanted people to look at the flowing patterns on the tiles and not at the building itself.

The dome of this mosque is covered with 1.5 million tiles. The inside of the roof and both minarets were also tiled.

Alhambra Palace

The arches were carved and covered with gold.

Muslim armies also conquered most of Spain. They built this palace, called the Alhambra.

It was built in southern Spain for a Muslim prince and took 200 years to finish.

27

Buildings of the East

Some of the most beautiful buildings in the world are in Asia. Three different religions have been important there over the centuries. They are Hinduism, Buddhism and the Muslim faith. Each one had its own building style.

The Taj Mahal

In 1526, people called the Moguls set up an Empire in India. They were Muslims.

The Empress Mumtaz Mahal died in 1620. Her husband, the Emperor built this tomb for her. It is called the Taj Mahal, which means 'crown of the palace'.

Hindu temple

Hindus believe that their gods live in the Himalaya Mountains. They built very tall temples to feel nearer to them.

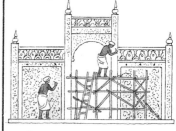

white tiles

The sculptors carved small hollows into the marble on decorated parts of the Taj Mahal. They then slotted a jewel into each one.

The Empress was actually buried in an underground chamber.

The Emperor was buried next to his wife in the Taj Mahal in 1658.

Twenty thousand men worked for 18 years to build the Taj Mahal.

The rich carving shows that Hindu builders worked on the Taj Mahal.

scaffolding

sikhara

The tower of a Hindu temple is covered with hundreds of colourful sacred carvings. It is called a sikhara.

Buddhist shrines

thorana

There are four carved gateways, called thorana, which lead into the stupa's courtyard.

About 1,500 years ago, some people in India began following the prophet Buddha. They built mounds called stupas, where they worshipped him. Most were brick, covered with white plaster, but some also had a thin layer of gold.

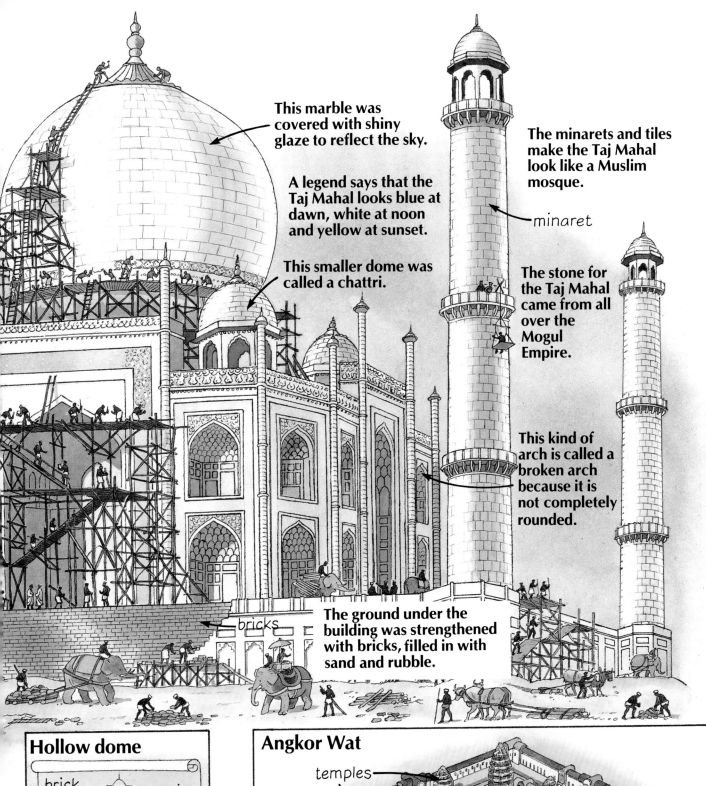

This marble was covered with shiny glaze to reflect the sky.

A legend says that the Taj Mahal looks blue at dawn, white at noon and yellow at sunset.

This smaller dome was called a chattri.

The minarets and tiles make the Taj Mahal look like a Muslim mosque.

minaret

The stone for the Taj Mahal came from all over the Mogul Empire.

This kind of arch is called a broken arch because it is not completely rounded.

bricks

The ground under the building was strengthened with bricks, filled in with sand and rubble.

Hollow dome

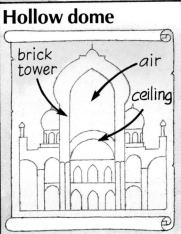

brick tower

air

ceiling

The dome of the Taj Mahal is hollow. It rests on a tower of bricks above the ceiling of the tomb.

Angkor Wat

temples

This city is called Angkor Wat. It was built 800 years ago by people called the Khmers. Travelling merchants probably told the Khmers about Hindu temple towers in India. The Khmers copied the style. They built tall temples as well.

Kings and palaces

Around 500 years ago, kings in Europe were very rich and powerful. Some built huge expensive palaces.

The Palace of Versailles

The most powerful king in Europe was Louis XIV of France. He reigned for 72 years, between 1643 and 1715.

His palace in the town of Versailles, 20km outside Paris, is one of the biggest palaces ever built.

Life at Versailles

The king wanted to control the powerful nobles in France. He made most of them live at the palace with him.

When the king got up in the morning, specially chosen nobles gave him his clothes. This was a great honour.

The nobles at Versailles danced at balls, played cards, or went to the opera house or theatre in the palace.

Louis' architects loved rich decoration. Nothing was plain.

This is the Galerie des Glaces (Hall of Mirrors). One wall is completely covered with mirrors.

Almost 3,000 men worked on the building site. They often worked through the night.

There were no proper toilets at the palace. It was often very smelly.

Water problems at Versailles

The king ordered 30,000 soldiers from his armies to build the aqueduct.

The palace had 1,400 fountains. A machine was built to pump water from the River Seine but it did not work.

Louis' men began building an aqueduct to carry water from a river 45km away. It was so difficult that they gave up.

The road from Paris was built to point directly to the King's bedroom.

Louis was called the 'Sun King'. He said he was as powerful as the sun. This picture from the palace shows his face surrounded by sun rays.

Many of the floors and walls were big slabs of coloured marble.

It took 47 years to finish Versailles.

Over 1,500 servants lived in the palace.

Versailles was the most expensive building of its time.

People were allowed into the palace to watch the king eat.

No one could solve the water problem. The fountains at Versailles only ever worked at certain times of each day.

A Spanish palace

There were also a church, a monastery and a college inside the palace walls.

The Escorial is built mainly of huge blocks of hard rock called granite.

Spain had colonies in the East which made it rich. Spain's king, Philip II, built this palace, called the Escorial.

It was quite dark and plain inside. Philip was very religious and did not want his palace to be too luxurious.

Russia

Until 1450, the huge nation now known as Russia was divided up into small areas or states. Each one had a capital city and its own ruler. There were plenty of forests full of wood for building. Stone was not used in most areas until centuries later.

Wooden towns

There were many fires.

frame

The first Russian builders were skilful carpenters. They used very simple tools to cut wood into the right size for all types of buildings.

For centuries, many towns were completely made of wood. Wooden walls surrounded them, and the roads were paved with logs.

In some towns, people bought ready-made house frames. They chose a frame, took it to where they wanted to live and then put it together.

Byzantine builders

About 600 years ago, the Roman Empire was split into two. The Eastern half became the Byzantine Empire, with Constantinople as its capital city.

Domes were often covered with paintings inside.

The walls were made of stone and brick, covered with plaster.

Russian builders went to Constantinople to learn how the Byzantines built and decorated their churches. When they returned home, they copied the style of domes and paintings they had seen.

A Russian cathedral

Muslim tribesmen called Tartars ruled most of Russia for almost 300 years from 1237.

Ivan, the ruler of Muscovy state, defeated the Tartars in 1552. He built this cathedral in his capital city, Moscow.

The colourful domes were added about 100 years later.

This is an icon. Icons were religious pictures painted on wood. They were hung on the cathedral walls.

Legend says that Ivan blinded the cathedral's two architects so that they could never build another one like it.

This type of roof is called a tent roof.

The cathedral is known as 'St Basil the Blessed', because Ivan's favourite adviser, Basil, is buried in it.

Its proper name is the Cathedral of the Virgin of the Intercession by the Moat.

These are called 'onion' domes, because of their shape.

The cathedral was built in an area in the centre of Moscow called the Kremlin.

The walls were made of brick and covered with blocks of stone.

Peter the Great

In 1689, the ruler of Russia was called Peter the Great. He wanted to build a city as great as any in Europe. Peter went to England and Holland and worked with craftsmen there. He brought architects and artists back to Russia.

Canals helped drain water away from the marshy site.

They planned a new city on marshes near the mouth of the River Neva. The peasant builders worked under terrible conditions, and many died. Peter called his city St Petersburg. It is now called Leningrad.

Wooden domes

Russian domes were specially shaped to stop snow piling up on them.

In forested areas, carpenters copied the style of stone churches, using wood.

The Winter Palace

Peter's daughter, the Empress Elizabeth, built this palace in St Petersburg in 1762. An Italian architect called Rastrelli was in charge of planning its 1,500 luxurious rooms.

33

Curves and columns

In the 1700s and 1800s, architects in Europe tried out all kinds of styles. Some preferred the simple columns and arches of Ancient Greece and Rome. Others covered their buildings with carving and rich decorations. People called planners became important in many cities. They built wide roads and large houses for the wealthy people.

Garden palace

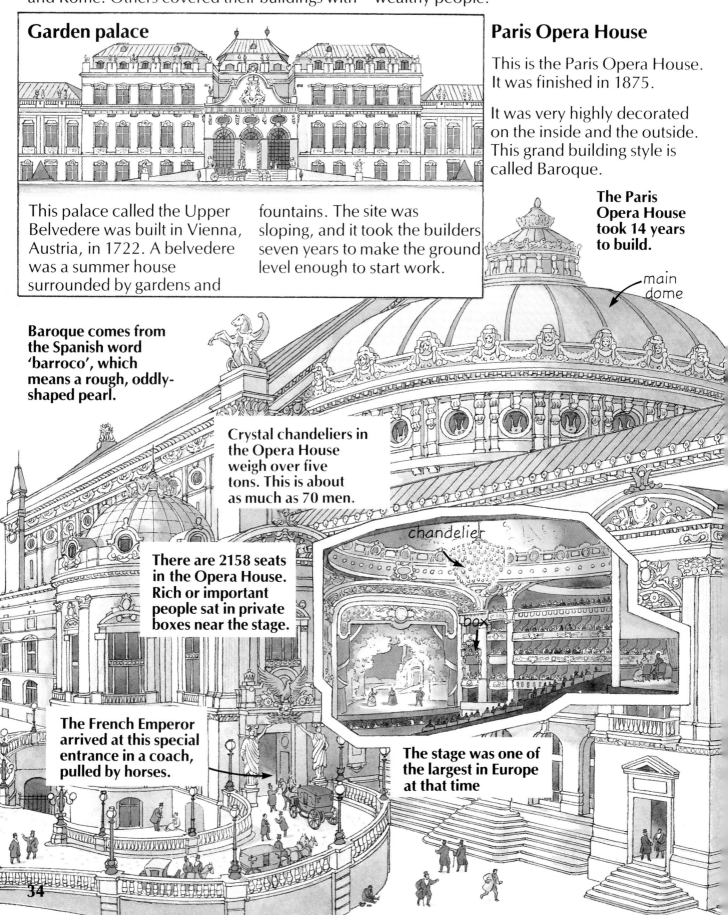

This palace called the Upper Belvedere was built in Vienna, Austria, in 1722. A belvedere was a summer house surrounded by gardens and fountains. The site was sloping, and it took the builders seven years to make the ground level enough to start work.

Paris Opera House

This is the Paris Opera House. It was finished in 1875.

It was very highly decorated on the inside and the outside. This grand building style is called Baroque.

The Paris Opera House took 14 years to build.

main dome

Baroque comes from the Spanish word 'barroco', which means a rough, oddly-shaped pearl.

Crystal chandeliers in the Opera House weigh over five tons. This is about as much as 70 men.

chandelier

box

There are 2158 seats in the Opera House. Rich or important people sat in private boxes near the stage.

The French Emperor arrived at this special entrance in a coach, pulled by horses.

The stage was one of the largest in Europe at that time

Terraces

In the 1700s, many people wanted to live in the towns and cities. Land to build houses on was scarce.

This row of houses is called the Royal Crescent.

The architect added Roman-style columns to make the row look like one building.

In the English city of Bath, houses were joined together into one long row, called a terrace. Each house had several floors of rooms, but did not take up much land.

Rich and fashionable people liked to be seen at the opera.

The architect, J.L.C. Garnier, won a competition to build the Opera House in 1861.

The road leading to the Opera House had no trees along its sides. This was to give people a clear view of the building.

O ACADEMIE NATIONALE DE MU

The staircase was the most richly decorated part of the Opera House.

Rococo

A style of decoration even richer than Baroque was popular in Europe in the 1700s. It was called Rococo.

It had lots of curls and curves, painted gold. Ceilings and walls had delicate, light paintings on them.

Stucco

stucco

Rococo decorators worked with a mixture called stucco. Stucco was usually made of ground stone, burnt chalk, water and animal hair.

Sculptors pasted wet stucco onto the wall. Then they carved it into different shapes. When it was dry, they covered it with gold paint.

North American builders

In the 1600s, people from all over Europe set sail to start new lives in North America. The first settlers landed on the east coast in 1607. Some travelled to the forests in the north, or set up huge farms called plantations in the south. Later, some went west across the plains. They used wood for all types of building at first.

Building a log cabin

Most log cabins only had one room.

The roof was made of thin slices of wood called shingles.

The gaps between logs were filled with moss.

In the forested areas in the north settlers used whole tree trunks to build log cabins.

They cut notches in the logs and slotted them together at the corners. Swedish settlers probably taught these skills. They had learnt them in forests in Sweden.

The White House

This is the White House in Washington DC. The President of the United States lives here.

The architects copied the grand style of European buildings at the time.

Building work began in 1792. The first President lived there in 1800, but the White House was still not finished.

Over 1.5 million tourists look around the White House every year.

The White House has been damaged by fire several times. Builders have replaced most of its wooden beams with steel ones.

This is the most important room in the White House. It is called the Oval Office. The President holds meetings and makes decisions here.

This is the President's swimming pool.

Many presidents have planted a tree in the gardens around the White House.

This is the Oval Office.

Clap-boarding

Chimneys in wooden houses had to be stone to stop them catching fire.

The planks all overlapped to keep rain out.

Settlers on the east coast often covered the frames of their houses with planks of wood. This was called clap-boarding.

The Capitol

The settlers set up 13 colonies. Britain ruled them until 1776, when they became the independent United States of America.

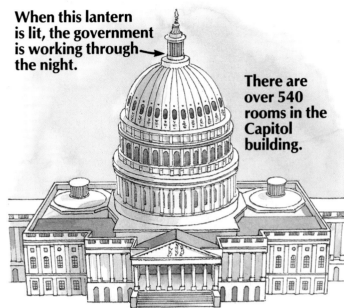

When this lantern is lit, the government is working through the night.

There are over 540 rooms in the Capitol building.

They needed buildings for their new government. This is the Capitol building, where the American government meets to decide laws. It was finished in 1867.

This room is called the Blue Room, because the carpets and decorations are all blue.

The President and his family live in these rooms on the second floor.

This is a small theatre for films and shows.

These white columns were added after the White House was finished, to make it look grander.

State banquets are held in this room. There are seats for 140 guests.

This is the Red Room. The walls are covered with red satin. The President's wife often meets visitors here.

Metal and glass

During the 1800s, large amounts of a red earth called iron ore were dug out of mines in England. It was made into the metal iron, and later into steel. New factories which had metal machinery were built in cities. Steel railway lines carried new steam engines. Architects wanted to use iron for building with as well.

The Crystal Palace

A Great Exhibition of things from all over the world was held in London in 1851. A new building made of iron and glass was built for it. It was called the Crystal Palace.

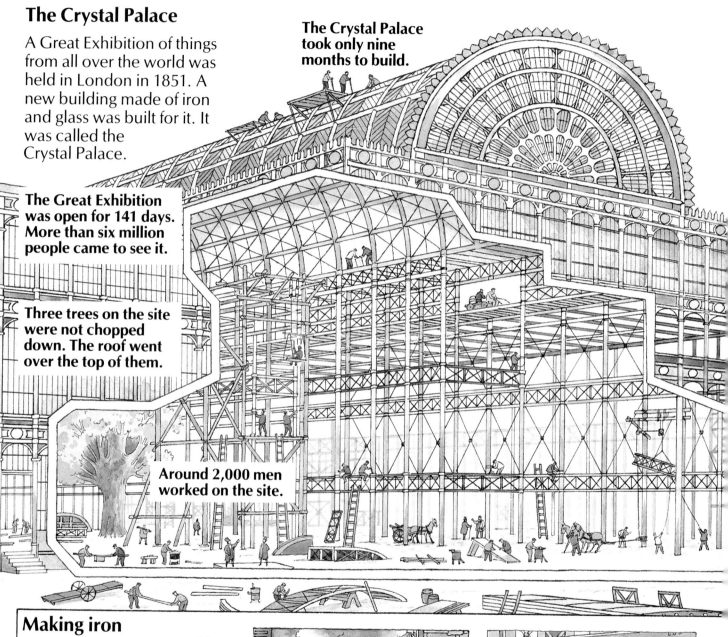

The Crystal Palace took only nine months to build.

The Great Exhibition was open for 141 days. More than six million people came to see it.

Three trees on the site were not chopped down. The roof went over the top of them.

Around 2,000 men worked on the site.

Making iron

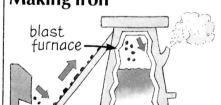

blast furnace

To make iron, iron ore, coke (a kind of coal) and limestone rock are put into a hot oven called a blast furnace. Hot air is blasted onto them.

cast

When the temperature is hot enough, the coke mixes with the iron ore to make liquid iron. This is poured into moulds, called casts.

bolt

The liquid cools and sets hard into cast iron. The pieces of iron are tipped out. They can now be fixed together with metal bolts.

Iron stations

Iron was used to build railway stations. This is the entrance to a Paris underground station. It was made from specially shaped pieces of cast iron in 1900.

The pieces of cast iron were made all over England and brought to the site by train.

Men rode on trolleys running in wooden grooves to put the glass panes into place. 80 men fitted 18,000 panes of glass in one week.

An architect called Thomas Paxton planned the Crystal Palace.

Iron bridge

This bridge was made in 1779 out of hundreds of pieces of cast iron bolted together. It was the first iron bridge ever built and it was soon copied by builders and engineers all over Europe.

The Eiffel Tower

Horse-drawn carriages brought the iron pieces from Eiffel's workshop, 1.5 km away.

The Tower is 300m high. This is about as tall as a 100 storey block of flats.

During the winter, the builders' fingers often froze to the metal bars, and the skin was pulled off.

The Tower sways in high winds but its iron parts do not snap.

The Great Exhibition in the Crystal Palace was very successful. Others were held all over the world. Gustav Eiffel built this tower in Paris for the Great Exhibition of 1889.

The Eiffel Tower was made of thousands of pieces of iron. They form a strong metal frame. It was the tallest building in the world at that time.

Modern buildings

At the end of the 1800s, builders began to use a new metal which was stronger than iron. It was called steel. Today, most big buildings are made of steel and concrete.

Building a skyscraper

The tallest buildings are called skyscrapers. They have to be built on a strong base, called a foundation.

A machine drills holes into the ground. These are filled with steel rods and concrete to make 'legs' called piles.

Skyscrapers have a frame made of steel bars, called girders. The girders are fixed together on top of the piles.

The builders pour concrete over criss-crossed steel rods to make the floors and the roof of the skyscraper.

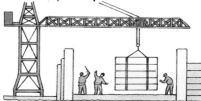

Huge cranes lift sheets of glass or metal that make the walls of skyscrapers today. They cover the steel frame.

The Empire State Building

Most early skyscrapers were built in America. This is the Empire State Building in New York. It took only a year to build and was finished in 1932.

It has a steel frame, filled in with over 10 million bricks. Blocks of limestone and strips of metal cover the outside walls.

When lifts were invented in 1857, people could travel between floors in high buildings more easily.

In 1945, an aeroplane crashed into the Empire State Building. It caused one million pound's worth of damage.

The Empire State Building has 102 floors of offices.

There are 1,860 steps from the top to the bottom.

The building went up by four and a half storeys each week.

The building has 6,500 windows.

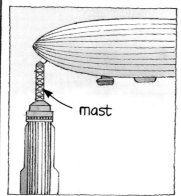

mast

This mast on top of the building was for airships to tie up to. But only two airships ever docked here.

The Pompidou Centre

This is the Pompidou Centre in Paris. It has five floors full of museums, theatres, cinemas and libraries. It was finished in 1979.

Most of its steel frame, the lifts, escalators and heating pipes are on the outside.

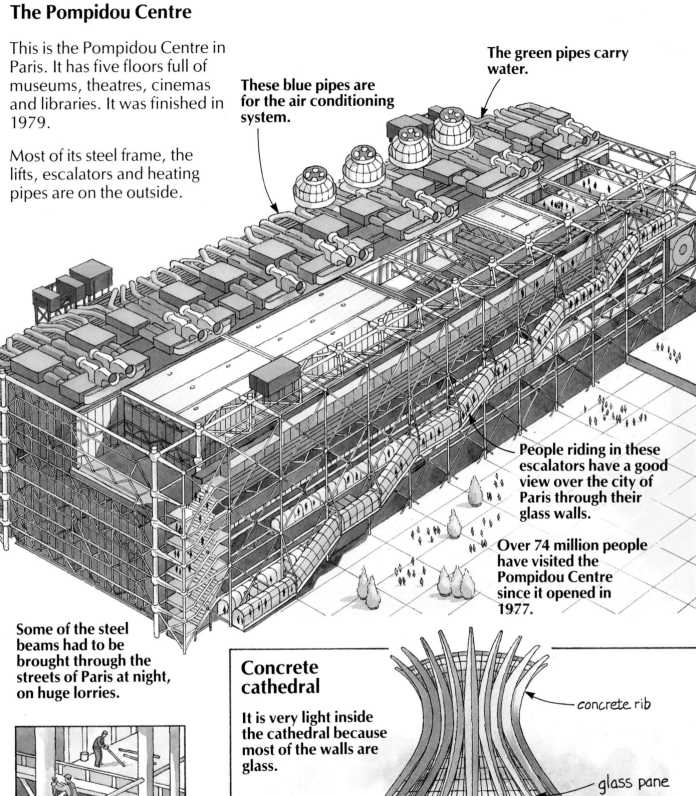

These blue pipes are for the air conditioning system.

The green pipes carry water.

People riding in these escalators have a good view over the city of Paris through their glass walls.

Over 74 million people have visited the Pompidou Centre since it opened in 1977.

Some of the steel beams had to be brought through the streets of Paris at night, on huge lorries.

A piece of steel called a gerberette joins the beams and columns together. They weigh as much as two elephants.

Concrete cathedral

It is very light inside the cathedral because most of the walls are glass.

concrete rib

glass pane

This cathedral is in Brasilia, the capital of Brazil. It was finished in 1970. It has 16 concrete ribs which make the shape of a crown. Glass panes fill the gaps between them and the roof is a huge block of concrete 12m wide.

Unusual buildings

Here are some of the world's most unusual buildings. They were all built at different times in history.

Sydney Opera House

This picture shows the Opera House in Sydney, Australia being built. Its strange-shaped roofs were very difficult to put into place.

It was finished in 1973.

The Opera House is built on top of a huge concrete platform in Sydney harbour.

The platform is supported by hundreds of concrete pillars. Some of these go down 13m into the mud.

The roofs of the Opera House are covered with over a million white and light brown tiles.

The architect of the Opera House won a competition with his amazing plan for the building.

The House of Bones

This block of flats in Barcelona, Spain is called the Casa Batló, which means the House of Bones. The bone-shaped pillars, skull-like balconies and scaly walls were added to the front of the building in 1907, by the architect Gaudí.

Rock church

11 churches like this one were built in the city of Lalibela, in Ethiopia.

This Christian church in Ethiopia, Africa was built out of a cube of solid rock over 700 years ago. The tribesmen cut the rock into the shape of a cross with simple hand tools.

The main opera theatre is under this roof. It has seats for 2,700 people.

One of the biggest cranes in the world was used to lift the huge pieces of the concrete roof.

The roofs are made of concrete ribs, with steel wire running through them. They are held together by pulling the wire tight and tying it.

Today there is a restaurant here.

Cave temple

This picture is looking into the temple from the door.

This is a cave temple in India. It was hollowed out of solid rock over 2,000 years ago. The builders only used simple tools. The temples were very dark inside as there was only one window above the door.

Tiny homes

Inside a flat.

Land is very scarce for building in Tokyo, Japan. This tower, built in 1972, contains tiny cube-shaped flats. Each flat has one room to cook, sleep and live in and a tiny bathroom.

Time Line

First huts over 300,000 years ago.

Mud mixed with straw to make bricks over 10,000 years ago.

Pyramids built in Egypt 5,000 years ago.

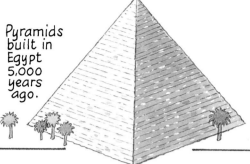

Ancient Greek columns had 3 styles called orders, about 2,500 years ago.

Holy mounds called stupas built in Asia, about 2,500 years ago.

Ancient Romans used concrete in building 2,000 years ago.

Tiles decorated Muslim buildings from about 800 years ago.

Stone castles built mainly in Europe. Around 700 years ago.

Cathedral ceilings had stone ribs. 700 years ago.

Incas in Peru built cities with stone blocks. From 400 years ago.

In the 1600s, Mogul rulers in India used Hindu and Muslim building styles.

Bricks filled in timber framed buildings. Around 300 years ago.

City planning started in Europe. Houses joined into one row called a terrace in the 1700s.

Iron used for building from 200 years ago.

Steel discovered in 1856.

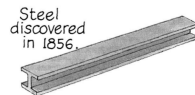

Stone columns supported roofs in Egyptian temples.

Ziggurats in Mesopotamia, 4,500 years ago.

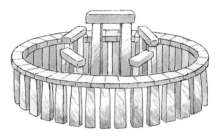

Europeans dragged stones into circles about 4,000 years ago.

Chinese and Japanese builders used brackets in roofs. From about 1,500 years ago.

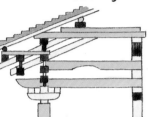

Hindus carved stone temples. From over 1,000 years ago.

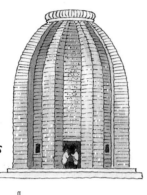

Muslims built mosques from about 1,000 years ago.

Stone masons worked on cathedrals in European cities.

The double dome of Florence Cathedral in Italy was built over 500 years ago.

Timber-framed buildings in Europe, from 500 years ago.

Thousands of men built huge palaces for European kings. From 1500 onwards.

Settlers in America built log cabins. From 300 years ago.

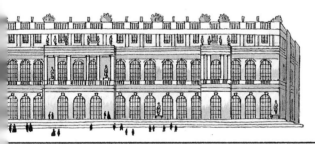

Rich decoration used in Europe, around 250 years ago.

Steel rods covered with concrete make floors from 70 years ago.

Buildings had over 100 floors from the 1930s.

Today, some buildings have their frame on the outside.

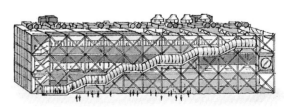

Glossary

Amphitheatre: arena surrounded by rows of seats.

Arch: upward-curving line of wedge-shaped stones or bricks between two walls.

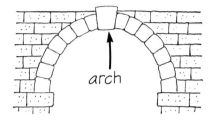
arch

Architect: person who designs and draws the plans for a building.

Bailey: area inside the wooden fence or stone wall of a castle.

Beam: long, straight piece of wood, **concrete** or steel. Used in roofs or to support floors.

Brick: block of mud and straw or baked clay. They are laid on top of each other in layers with **mortar** between them to make walls.

Cement: first made by burning limestone and grinding it into a powder. Today it is made by burning a mixture of chalk or limestone and clay. It sets hard when mixed with water.

Chisel: metal tool with special blade for cutting wood or stone into the right shape and size.

Column: a thick stone pole or pillar. Rows of columns support slabs of stone or wooden beams laid across them.

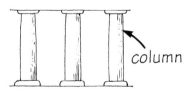
column

Concrete: mixture of small stones, sand, **cement** (burnt chalk and clay), and water.

Crane: machine for lifting heavy things to higher levels. Probably first invented by the Romans.

Crenellations: gaps in the top of a castle's turrets and the tops of walls for firing at enemies through.

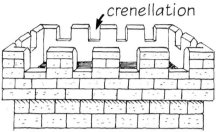
crenellation

Cruck: single curved tree trunk split into two and used in a timber-framed house.

Daub: mud or clay mixed with straw and smeared on to walls to bind layers of twigs (**wattle**) together.

Dome: curved roof over a building.

Drawbridge: bridge over the **moat** of a castle. It can be raised or lowered.

Fluting: grooves cut into **columns** from top to bottom.

Flying buttress: a stone or brick prop that takes some of the weight of a particularly high wall.

flying buttress

Foundation: strong base on which a building rests.

Gargoyles: carved stone figures with holes which rainwater flows off roofs through.

Girder: long, straight piece of metal, usually steel. Used in modern buildings.

Half-timbered: a building with a wooden frame, filled in with **plaster**, **bricks** or **wattle** and **daub**.

Henge: circle of blocks of stone or wood built by prehistoric men.

Icon: sacred picture inside churches built in the Byzantine style. They were often rich colours such as red or gold.

Iron: metal made from red earth called iron ore which has been heated in a furnace.

Keep: main building, often a tower, inside the walls of a castle.

Lath: long, thin strips of wood, usually covered with **plaster** or **daub** to make walls.

Lintel: block of stone, wood or steel laid flat across the top of two upright blocks or a gap between two walls. A flat arch.

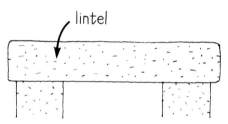
lintel

Mason: person who cuts and shapes stone for buildings.

Mihrab: holiest place in a mosque. A decorated nook which points towards Mecca.

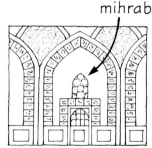
mihrab

Minaret: tower of a mosque.

Moat: ditch filled with water around a castle.

Mortar: first made by burning and grinding limestone into a powder and adding sand and water. Now it is usually made of **cement**, sand and water. It is put between blocks of stone and **bricks**.

Mosaic: picture made up of many small pieces of pottery or glass set into **mortar**.

Motte: mound of earth on which early European castles were built.

Nave: main part of a church or cathedral which leads up to the altar.

Nogging: bricks laid in patterns between pieces of wood in a timber-framed building.

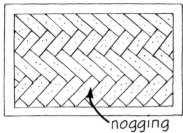

nogging

Pagoda: sacred Buddhist tower. Built of wood, stone or **bricks**.

Pargetting: patterns made by scraping special tools and moulds over wet plaster on walls.

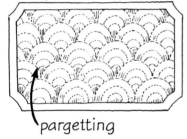

pargetting

Pick: small, pointed tool for cutting stone into the right size and shape.

Pile: 'leg' of timber, steel or **concrete** with metal rods through it. Used as **foundation** for some large buildings.

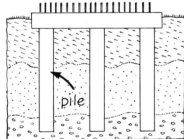

pile

Pinnacle: pointed, richly carved decoration on top of towers and **buttresses**.

Plaster: first made by burning limestone into powder and adding sand and water. Now it is usually made of powdered gypsum rock mixed with sand and water.

Portcullis: castle gate made of thick bars of wood or metal with spikes along the bottom. It can be raised or lowered.

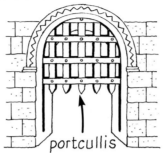

portcullis

Quarry: place where stone is dug out of the ground.

Reinforced concrete: concrete with steel rods running through it to strengthen it.

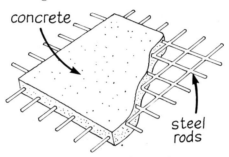

concrete

steel rods

Roof bosses: carved wood or stone ornaments on church and cathedral ceilings.

Scaffolding: framework of poles with ladders and platforms to help builders reach every level of a building.

Shell keep: wall around the buildings of an early castle.

Shingles: small slices of wood used to cover roofs and some walls.

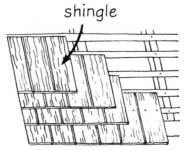

shingle

Shrine: place where a god is worshipped.

Sikhara: carved tower of a Hindu temple.

Spire: tall, pointed tower on top of churches and cathedrals.

Stave churches: churches made completely of wood. They were mainly built in Scandinavia.

Stucco: moulded **plaster**, often painted gold. Sometimes spread on to the outside of buildings.

Stupa: sacred Buddhist mound, usually built of layers of **bricks**.

Tatami: bamboo mats covering the floor in Japanese houses.

Terrace: row of houses joined together.

Thatch: bundles of straw or reeds used to make roofs for houses.

Tile: thin slice of baked clay, usually used to cover roofs. Painted tiles often covered the roof and walls of Islamic buildings.

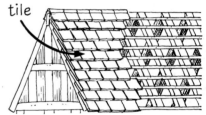

tile

Tracery: small pieces of cut stone which make a pattern when fixed together. Often used in cathedral windows.

Vault: an arched roof. If a vault is divided into sections by stone ribs, it is called a ribbed vault.

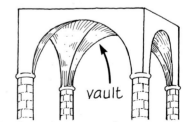

vault

Wattle: twigs woven between pieces of wood and plastered with mud.

Ziggurat: mud-brick mound with a temple on the top layer. Built in ancient middle eastern countries such as Sumer and Assyria.

Index

First published in 1991 by Usborne Publishing Ltd, Usborne House, 83-85 Saffron Hill, London, EC1 8RT London.
This edition published by in 1998 by Tiger Books International PLC, Twickenham.
Printed in Hong Kong / China. ISBN 1-85501-998-1